POWER PHONING

POWER PHONING

By Michael Friedman and Jeffrey Weiss

ISBN: 0-8081-0156-0

POWER PHONING
was prepared and produced by
Tern Enterprises, Inc.
Sagaponack Road
Bridgehampton, New York 11932

Cover Designer: Michael Soha

Typography by Paragraphics, Inc.

Cover color separation by Hong Kong Scanner Craft Company Ltd.

Printed and bound in Hong Kong by Leefung-Asco Printers Ltd.

Produced for
Woodbury Press

Contents

The Philosophy of Power Sell

The Power Sell series is based on a simple, exciting truth: **You, the individual salesman, are better at your profession than you think you are.**

Sure, there are some selling tips you might not know about yet—and they're here by the score, scattered helpfully throughout the six Power Sell books.

But the bottom-line message that makes Power Selling work for so many successful, high-income salesmen is directed straight at *you.*

First of all, together we're going to **find the specific strengths and specific weaknesses** that make you the unique salesman you are.

Next we're going to show you how you can **turn up the power** *full blast* on those characteristic strengths: how to focus on what you do best; how to aim for the most productive use of your talents; how to intensify, with pride and passion, the qualities that naturally brought you into the challenging and rewarding profession of selling.

Then we'll talk about dealing with those **qualities that might look like weaknesses.** Power Selling is an approach based on facing the truth: how to turn negative factors, once recognized, into powerfully positive qualities; how to take command of the sales situation so that strong, not weak, points will take control; how to play to your strengths.

These are books about getting *influence,* and making it work for you. About getting the customer to take his buying cues from you. About bringing customer interest to a white-hot boil. And about **turning selling into cooperation**—with the customer eager for you to help him buy.

It works! It can put you in control of that vital element, the sales close. And that, in turn, can change your career—and your ideas about yourself. So turn the page, and see how power—in its most positive sense—will put **you** at the top!

INTRODUCTION

Just how good are you? Say you're an ace at the face-to-face encounter. And you know how to get across a whole novel in right-on body language. You've learned how to get maximum power from the gifts you have for successful salesmanship.

Fine. But this is the last quarter of the twentieth century, and the personal contact is becoming more extinct with every passing day. A few salespeople still work door-to-door, and thousands work in salesrooms, of course, and personal contact is the secret of much selling on the road—*but,* between you and the customer, there is likely to be a machine, at least half the time.

We're not talking just about telephone sales, which is a specialized skill. **We're talking about all sales, and it's the telephone through which you seek out prospects on a hot tip.** When you want to set up meetings or trigger the memories of a customer you pleased in the past, you usually go to the phone.

With the telephone, you hopscotch across the country, chasing down leads. You have to get information for a customer, and that's not always a piece of cake. You have to deal with repairmen or vice-presidents, bankers or deliverymen—and all of these telephone contacts require the same kind of vigor you bring to personal encounters.

But look at the disadvantages, from the salesperson's point of view:

- **The other guy doesn't have a face,** so you can't use your skills in reading his thoughts and psyching out his unconscious motives. . .

- **You don't have a face, either,** so some of the charm and persuasive power you've developed is suddenly diminished. Whether your style is based upon the wide grin or the friendly wink, a sympathetic smile or a sober look of concentration, it's lost over the telephone wires—at least, for the near future. . .

- **You can't reach out and touch,** never mind what the ads claim. You can't use body language, or clap someone on the shoulder (*if* that's your natural style); you can't gesture to a fine point, or touch a soft blanket. You are, quite literally, only a disembodied voice, and you're in danger of becoming sound without substance. . .

- **You don't control the setting.** In Power Selling, you always want to be in control of the situation. You are the director. You are, in a word, the manipulator. But how do you achieve that end over the telephone, when you don't know who is in the room, or what effect the room is having on the mood of the person on the other end of the line?

With all these disadvantages, from the traditional point of view, how can a Power Salesperson make effective use of the telephone?

And remember: The telephone's only the beginning. With other devices, you may find yourself no longer talking with someone but "interfacing." *Today, messages are more and more frequently transmitted between two or more people sitting at computer termi-*

nals. You don't even have the use of that instrument you've developed for your own ends over the years: your unique and flexible voice. How do you take charge of the action when all you have at your command are the words upon a screen?

Rule: *Don't let technology become a barrier.*

Electronic devices are springing up everywhere, just as the telephone did, because of one thing: *efficiency.* Electronic communication is efficient because of its speed (the speed of light, and you will never beat that), and its accuracy, which should be 100%, if all parties are alert and listening to one another.

Be grateful for the speed and accuracy. Take them for granted...*but compensate.*

The loss, in telephonic communication, is in personal appeal—expression, gesture, movement, intimate contact, physical sharing. You must compensate for that.

The gain, aside from the efficiency, is concentration on the voice, on what is being said and how it sounds.

In other words, one of your most important tools, usually just a part of your kit, has to become your most important tool. What you have expressed before in other ways has to be powerfully compressed into the voice alone. It has to have gestures, and it has to make your expressions. It has to tease out responses.

And it has to set the context of the relationship between you and the customer or prospect, whether or not the two of you will ever see each other face to face.

Power Phoning is a completely separate technique of selling, even though the aims are, as always in sales:

- To project yourself powerfully into the potential of the situation;
- To be ready to take advantage of each gain you make; and
- To take your customer or prospect in the direction that will work to mutual benefit.

Let's look at the secrets of that critical aspect of Power Selling: Power Phoning.

CHAPTER ONE
You Are Your Voice

For Power Phoning, your voice has to radiate self-confidence, but it cannot have an abrasive or piercing timbre. It has to be capable of warmth, but avoid smarm. It has to be light, when that's what's needed, and clearly to the point when you are conveying factual information.

It has to be a portrait of you in sound.

Remember when you took assessment of yourself to begin Power Selling? You played to your strengths, worked to eliminate weaknesses. You decided for yourself what kinds of sales techniques were true to your talents and your personality. You didn't make the mistake of copying gestures, or expressions, or attitudes that were not powered naturally from within you.

The same approach is necessary for developing your phone personality. Think about it.

- You *are* how you *sound.*
- They *meet* what they *hear.*
- The *salesroom* is the *customer's head.*

To take over the atmosphere of that salesroom, you have to work hard to ensure that, over the telephone line, your voice resounds with the same uniqueness of personality that you carry when you walk into a sales situation.

Should it be deep? Should it be flippant? Should it sound like Robert Redford?

It should be **you.**

Work with a tape recorder; they're dirt cheap these days, and they're so portable that you can turn to them wherever you are, whenever there's a spare moment.

Take the advice of professional actors. The first time you hear your voice on tape, resist cardiac arrest. Unless you're one of the world's happiest egoists, you won't be completely pleased with the sound. "Is that me?" is the reaction of most people. And a great many people, as you know, cannot bear to hear themselves on tape, even when they love seeing themselves on videotape or film. Why? Because with films, one is able to come across with all the resources of personality, just as the salesperson does in the one-on-one sales encounter. With sound tape, one is restricted to that one resource, just like the salesperson on the telephone.

But you don't have the luxury of turning off the machine just because your voice doesn't please you. You have a challenge—the challenge of working on it, of making improvements, and developing control.

BREAK DOWN THE VOICE ON PAPER

List the good points, and the weak. And be honest with yourself—not too self-conscious, not too willing to ignore possible faults. Aim for the positive as well as the negative. If you sound too rushed, or don't clearly pronounce certain consonants, make a note. . . but also be sure to note that you have a sincere and pleasing lilt in your delivery, or that your natural pitch has a compelling warmth.

Learn to listen for how you look. Decide how to change the image to fit the real you, by emphasizing what is most personal in your voice and delivery.

Ask for advice from a stranger or from an enemy, or from a voice professional (anybody but a friend). The first thing you have to learn is that your voice probably sounds worse to you than to anyone else, because you have false expectations. You may have thought, for example, it was a dark baritone of some character, but a tape shows that you muddy the effect by pronouncing indistinctly. Yet an unbiased observer—that is, listener —can help you with a balanced assessment. They don't have your expectations; they should be more able to hear what is really there.

When you identify the strengths and weaknesses of your voice, take the sensible approach to improvement:

> *Don't worry about what cannot or*
> *should not be changed overnight,*
> *and get right to work on what can*
> *be improved with practice.*

A strong regional accent will take quite a bit of time and effort to eradicate, but noisy breathing habits, or a tendency to drop pitch at the end of every sentence, or a problem with clearly pronounced s's are easier to concentrate on right away.

You're not an actor, you say?

Nonsense! You must hone your tools to their sharpest. And the First-Impression Rule works on the telephone just as it does in the flesh. **The first impression is the strongest impression.** Sure, you can overcome it, but why hamstring yourself that way? It takes you quite a while to build up serious respect on the sales floor, if you make your entrance by slipping on a banana peel. If you begin a telephone conversation with a nasal whine, you will probably never get past the unpleasant entrance.

Yes, that's what your first word is—an entrance. What the other guy hears is what he sees. To him, as we've said, that voice is *you.*

DOUBLE YOUR ETIQUETTE QUOTIENT

You not only have to realize what people expect from a polite telephone conversation—and there *are* some strict rules—but you also have to realize, if you have a national market, that:

> *Telephone etiquette is different*
> *in various regions of the country.*

What sounds businesslike in Manhattan, for example, may be thought rude in Jackson, Mississippi. On the other hand, the slow build of a phone conversation in the Midwest may be taken as time-wasting or even sarcastic by a hard-pressed business professional in a hard-driving urban center on the East or West Coast.

These things you will have to learn from the locals. What's considered polite in one town may be considered less so across the river. Depend upon your ear, and keep listening for nuances.

But some rules are universal:

Identify yourself right away! Unless you're making an obscene phone call, there's no reason to keep your identity in reserve. Do you wear a mask when you enter the salesroom or visit a client in his office? There's nothing to be gained in anonymity. Trying to catch the customer off guard? There's no good reason to, and you just anger him by seeming to be shifty.

Let your voice paint the portrait, let your words give the details. You are somebody with a powerful message. Say so. Take the initiative. Don't hang back. Whether it's "Howdy" or "Hello" or "How's it hangin'?" that's considered the proper intro in your sales area, follow the greeting with, "This is Power Salesperson X." You may only want to say the words "Power Salesperson" to yourself, but say the rest loud, and say it clear.

And state your business: If a client's worth your time, he has not got much time. You have to take that attitude, anyway. Right off, in the way you come to the point, you're letting your man know that you think he's too important for time wasting. When you explain who you are and what you represent, you are signaling that you're in the mood for business. You will be wanting answers. You will be prepared to ask questions.

Name and purpose, politely and clearly stated—in those few seconds you have made a first impression. You have established the tone of the conversation; you

You Are Your Voice

are well on your way to setting the ground rules.

Whether talking to a receptionist or a CEO, you have to be in character—the image of the Power Salesperson. You've got to be so secure in your role that other people believe. Your voice has to project confidence, but more than that: you are someone with a job to do. You're not abrupt, but you are brief and to the point. You're friendly, but you don't waste time on long-winded pleasantries.

And all the time, you should have your antennae out. Even in the first minute or two of the conversation, you should be listening. You've got your script in your head, but you know that you have to tailor it for the individual encounter. When you're face to face with someone, it's easier. Over the telephone, though, you might have to take a few shots in the dark before the signals begin to clear up.

Which brings us to the next chapter on the importance of listening.

CHAPTER TWO
What You Hear Is What You Get

Learning to listen may sound like a passive act.

That's actually backwards thinking. Learning to listen is a *powerful* action; it is power held in reserve, and tamed to your ends, but it is real power nonetheless.

And the results! Over and over, you will hear successful salespeople say that their real secret is that they know how to listen. If you listen well, the customer might think you agree with him, or he might think that you are simply enthralled with the force of his thinking or the beauty of his language. He just feels good.

And don't we all? Anyone who listens to our point of view must be pretty smart, right?

The trouble with telephone sales is that you don't have facial cues to help you. Is there a pause because the customer is thinking of the right word? If you think not, then you'll probably interrupt him. But if you wait for him to speak, and he's waiting for you, he'll be made uneasy. And an embarrassed person is an angry person.

Language will give you clues, and a sense of regionalisms. In some parts of the country, a speaker will clearly come to a halt after making his point. In others, there may be one thought, a pause, and then a reworking of the thought, then a pause. . .and so on. It takes experience to hear these differences.

Rule: *He's listening to you, too!*

You can doff the passive role, when appropriate, and give your own sound cues. You can help the conversation go forward by avoiding misunderstandings. Make clear that you have finished a sentence. End it firmly. Or end with a question for your customer. Don't let him risk embarrassment by interrupting you because you haven't finished a thought or have left a sentence hanging in midair.

SILENCE IS NOT EMPTINESS

Work on identifying the various kinds of silence—that's where your powers will *really* come into full play.

Can you tell the difference between stunned silence and an angry burn? Between a moment when the customer doesn't know what to say, because he's thinking or confused, and a moment when the customer has had his attention diverted elsewhere and is simply not listening to you?

Out of context, there would be no way to tell the difference between these various silences, all of them blank in sound. But in *context,* you can learn to make very educated guesses. The character of a silence is determined by what has gone before and by what follows. You have to rely on intuition, and on experience.

It's more natural than you might think. And if you've been involved in the personal give-and-take of the sales experience, you already have most of the necessary skills.

The danger is that you may forget to use what you know.

Listen well to the *words*. Listen twice as attentively to the silences. That's where the action may be.

When it comes to the words, listen to *how* a thing is said, as well as to *what* is said. There are many kinds of "no," and many kinds of "yes." When you are face-to-face with someone, you can tell by gestures and other clues how to interpret his words. On the telephone, you have to listen to the expression in the voice.

Special clues:

- Are there subjects that the customer is clearly avoiding?
- Is there an ironic tone to his use of your product's name?
- Does he speak forthrightly, or does he hesitate?
- If you ask a direct question, is there a pause before the answer?
- Does he sound distracted, as if he's taking opinions from someone else?
- In the picture his voice makes in your mind, what is fuzzy? Missing? Contradictory?

You know what you need to know—you just have to turn sound into picture.

And don't forget what you learned at your mother's knee. "Please" and "Thank you" and "May I?" are much heavier on the phone. When you say them, you are heard. Every word is heavier, but courtesy words are especially so. And your interlocutor hears the tone behind them: sincerity, or lack of feeling—whichever's there.

Listen for the effect that your courtesy has upon the customer.

Show that you are being polite, not putting yourself down like a doormat, and he will respond with respect. Show that you understand that courtesy is the social form of the Golden Rule, and he will understand that you expect to be treated as you are treating him.

> *Courtesy, over the telephone,*
> *is a badge of honor.*

In the right tone of voice, it announces that you know the rules and you expect them to be followed.

To put it bluntly, *courtesy is your way of saying that you do not intend to be given short shrift.*

If you can behave with circumspection, so can your customer. You mean to conduct the conversation on a gentlemanly level, to use the old phrase, whether you are man or woman.

Listen closely, and you will hear him sizing you up: You've got the advantage on that score. He doesn't know what you look like, what you wear, or even your exact age. You've got him off-center on those points. Listen, as he tries to sound you out.

It works both ways. And if you're conscious of that, of the way the power game works on the telephone, you can take control of the whole conversation. You see, when you're listening closely, you're gathering information that's important for your purposes. But when *he* begins to listen, and you hear him listening, you can work your will.

The power in Power Phoning comes
from knowing how information
comes through the voice.

The power comes from being able to listen with profit
. . .and then understand how the listening to the listening can be even more profitable: When is he paying the
most attention? What does he ask? What parts of conversation cause him to pause before replying? When
does he reply without taking time to think—and when
does he take a long time to consider exactly how to ex-
press himself?

In his behavior are a thousand clues, but the best
come from your understanding of when the customer is
listening to you, and why.

YOU'RE NOT ON CANDID CAMERA

So, take notes. Document what you're learning as you
listen: Note down exactly what the customer is saying
to you.

Just a minute Wasn't sales telephoning supposed to
have all these disadvantages? Maybe. But it allows you
to concentrate on a few skills, while taking advantage of
some unique opportunities. You don't wave a pencil in
a customer's face. It would make him nervous, and
probably give him the idea that you can't remember
things very well.

The truth is, you can't—unless you're one in a mil-
lion. No one remembers very well, as any good defense

lawyer knows. Witnesses remember what never happened. And any reporter knows that certain public figures are certain that they've been misquoted, even after a tape of the exact wording has been played back to them.

We don't hear ourselves, and we can't take in everything someone else is saying, *and* remember it all— particularly when we have other things to be concerned about, like appearance and what we're going to say next.

DOODLE TO A CLOSE

But Power Phoning frees you to work with a pad. Did he say $3,000 ten minutes ago? You have the notes right in front of you. Did he say he's just come from having lunch at the Horse and Hounds on Cavanaugh Avenue? Bring it up later, or in a letter. Meanwhile, you're figuring the numbers that will help you deliver the goods to fit his needs, and you're ready when it's time to talk.

Simple technological tools, pencil and paper. But they can make for a very impressive telephone image. You're the salesperson who remembers what he's told and who can shift the numbers around to make them work for both of you.

But this is all achieved in the protective silence of the telephone situation.

You take the credit for prodigious memory. *You don't give the secret away!*

Which is more impressive? (A) "Yes, sir, you said

457 eyebolts; I know, because I noted it down when you said it" or (B) "The eyebolts you need, I believe you said 457 or so, can be. . ."

Can it be said too often? **We all love someone who listens to us.** And if a salesperson not only listens but also *remembers?* Well, the customer owes you something already.

So play this telephone advantage to the hilt.

> *Don't let anything important escape*
> *your pencil, and bring it up later in*
> *the conversation in a relevant way.*

Also, have all appropriate materials nearby, or a colleague or helper who can go search out information. If the customer says, "Well, we really wouldn't be able to make a decision until you searched up Facts I, II, and III," a Power Seller, with luck on his side, could have the manual nearby which contains Fact III, and throw a note to an assistant asking for Facts I and II, which can be obtained by another phone or from an expert down the hall. Before the conversation goes very far, you can say, "Well, sir, we have all the facts you said were necessary to make a decision, and here they are." **This is the kind of thing you can't do in person,** because, on the phone, the customer isn't aware of the process; he isn't getting his defenses in order.

In short, you can bowl him over.

Off guard, the customer will be primed for your next move, so close in. Over the telephone, you can marshal your resources without warning. This is a fine tactical advantage. Listen with the ears of a bat, but make sure that he doesn't understand your silences—that's the approach.

And remember: **What can't be seen isn't happening.** So don't give your secrets away. Don't let him know how you do it. Don't let him guess how you keep one jump ahead, with your trusty pencil and pad and your stacks and stacks of useful materials.

Work the shadows...

CHAPTER THREE
Out of Sight, Out of Range

Far away, but right next to you: that's the contradiction of the telephone and other communications devices. Someone is on the other side of the country, but the voice is perched in your ear.

We all live with this contradiction and think nothing of it. But we make assumptions about it that could weaken the thrust of your sales presentation. Unconsciously, part of you is probably saying, "Well, he's all the way out in California...not really my concern." No, you don't think that consciously, but the customer *is* far away. You've got to listen to the positive side of your nature, the part that says, "But, dammit, he's right here, and I've got him [his voice, anyway] clutched in my right hand."

He's in your hand, not a bit farther away than that.

Focus on him. You can move that voice back and forth. You could throw him against the wall, if that was your nature. He's in your power, as a sales prospect, and you have literally "got him on the line."

Okay, but he's not buying.

Are you going to let him get away with that?

Of course not! You're sure of what you want to sell, and you're sure of how it will fit into his business plans, and you know that you have the power to make this sell work.

What's holding it up?

GETTING THROUGH
WITH THE SMOKING GUN

You have to find the right key.

The deal's a good one, but the customer isn't taking the order. You know there's nothing wrong with the product—that's the attitude that powers a sale. You know, because you've done your research properly, that the customer *can* buy. You may have learned from listening closely that he's not happy with a current product or service.

What's wrong? Perhaps you haven't realized the necessity of giving him the "Smoking Gun."

You've explained why he should want the product, but perhaps you've forgotten that he works for someone else. He reports to a boss, who reports to a division head, who reports to a board.

The Smoking Gun is the evidence that your customer doesn't directly need, but that he needs for one of two very important reasons: to convince his superiors that his judgment is sound, before the fact, so that the sale will be approved...or to convince his superiors that his judgment *was* sound, after the fact, so he won't be made a scapegoat for problems elsewhere in the company.

Corporate politics, that's what we're talking. As a Power Seller, working most of the time on your own, you may forget just how rare and special your working independence has become. **Even heads of major corporations sometimes feel that their hands are tied**

these days, with the necessity to be responsible to stockholders and board members. Think how your customer, if he's in a large company, is caught between many contending factions.

He needs that evidence. But he may not ask for it. He may be too embarrassed to say, "Hey, you've sold me, but I need such-and-such to convince the higher-ups." You have to hear him say that between the lines, from thousands of miles away, and produce the Smoking Gun. Is it what he needs? You'll know in a moment. You must then give it to him; the sound you hear will be relief. . .with an appropriate tinge of gratitude.

THE ABSOLUTE WORST

The customer agrees that the product sounds perfect. He can't think of anything wrong with it. So why isn't he buying?

Intuition will have to be your guide, but maybe those strange silences over the telephone lines indicate that he needs to be told "The Absolute Worst." That's how the mind works, sometimes.

Something just sounds too good to be true. What you should have done (and will, the next time) is follow the old rule of bringing out the bad news first. The high cost, or the frequent repairs, or the likelihood of imminent obsolescence.

Of course, now, you're in a ticklish situation. You bring up The Absolute Worst, and the customer may ask, "Why didn't you bring this up before?" (And that question implies, "And how many other bad things do you have to tell me?")

But go ahead. Do it.

Your tactic? You seem to realize, all of a sudden, that something is holding your man back. You wonder if it could be the Absolute Worst, and if it is, you want him to know that there's another way of looking at it. That's the way *you* look at it, and so you don't even think about it as a disadvantage anymore. After all, people who come to your product have typically preferred its technical superiority, even with the occasional breakdowns, or have felt that the high cost could be amortized in ways that bring tax relief.

Pimples? **You don't cover them up, but you try to turn them to advantage.** After all, they're an indication of hormonal change, and a harbinger of the mature beauty that is to follow. Put the spotlight on them; admit they're there; show that there's something good to be said about them.

Maybe—we'd say, *probably*—the customer already knew about the disadvantage. He just wanted to see if you'd bring it up and how you'd handle it.

Deal with the Absolute Worst, and you'll be dealing with a new customer.

He's going to respect you, if you admit the defect and show how it can be put into reasonable perspective.

RING HIS DOORBELL

You suddenly realize that, unlike you, the customer thinks there's a continent between you. He doesn't realize you have him in the palm of your hand. He doesn't realize, in a nutshell, that you and your product are really as accessible as you claim.

You have to "Ring His Doorbell"—let him know you're as close as the front door.

You're not there on the doorstep, but what about your product? Has the company down the street been a good customer, or has someone in town good reason to praise your work? Is your company known for its work in the area?

> *Somehow, you have to plant the idea that your product is a reality, accessible to him...even if you're sitting miles away in a different time zone.*

There are too many unspoken assumptions—that the product is suited for your area, not for his...or that you are too far away to be responsible, in case something goes wrong. You have to relieve these assumptions, assumptions that won't be stated, but hidden beneath his words.

Perhaps he's the first in his area to try your service. Well, you can't avoid the truth. Since you can't emphasize accessibility, you might want to stress how unique he will be. Explain how important it is for the company to make this first inroad, and he'll get the point: You'll be going out of your way to make sure that, as the first buyer, he's happy with the product.

Or maybe you just have to know more about his town than he does. *Show him how the service is particularly good for him* because it works so well with the climate, or the transportation factors, or the tastes of the populace. (Of course, you never *tell* a man about his own area; you *remind* him, and show him what he already knows will fit into your sales picture.) If you've really got the time to do apt research, you can talk about how your product will help him avoid the problems of other companies in the area.

And remember: **You have that telephone advantage of being invisible, part of the electronic darkness.** You can have maps and reference books and atlases and newspaper articles right on your desk, for immediate reference.

Ring His Doorbell by knowing where he lives—as factually as possible.

Ring His Doorbell by showing him, in a sense, how to walk your product from the street and out of its packing crate and into full assembly-line order.

Ring His Doorbell, at the bottom line, by giving him the sense that you are in the room with him. You see the size and shape of his needs. You feel the full flavor of the town and its people. You understand the situation from his point of view and could take a walk in his boots.

BITE THE DOLLAR!

Everyone wants to bite the dollar, and see if it's really made of gold. Obviously, this is a difficult feat over the phone. You've got to come up with the second-best thing: the accumulation of physical evidence.

If it's in the paper, it must be true: Do you have news clips about your product? Good reports in trade magazines? Don't be shy about including small-town stories that cover the opening of your local offices. If it's in the paper, it has legitimacy. There's truth in the old saw: I don't care what they write about me, as long as they spell my name right.

If they can pay, they must be good: In reasonable amounts, mail your customer copies of ad campaigns, or send along the product descriptions that you use with other sales personnel. Emphasize the ads that have good clear photos and a straightforward product message. You don't want any interference with your own message...which is being tailor-made for this particular customer. Ads show that your company has made an investment in the product, that they're committed to it.

If the plug's good, the pumpkin must be ripe: You can't always send a sample of your product, but try an approach that your customer will never forget. What works depends upon you and your aims. Sometimes, to be sure, it *might* work to hire someone to appear on your customer's doorstep in a gorilla suit and present him with some object that brings your product to mind.

Usually, however, your creative approach will be more sober and more original. Perhaps a well-made toy will bring your product to mind, or a mounted machine part will suggest the engineering marvels of your product. Anything physical that is somehow a reminder of what you have to offer is a good supplement to your telephone campaign. It brings you into the room. It is an objective proof that you exist, but you have to power your way into many other levels of customer consciousness. *Objects jog the memory. They exist, you exist.*

OTHER BARRIERS

Each situation may introduce you to another hidden reason for customer resistance over the telephone. Always, you are translating your sales knowledge to the special challenges and restrictions of telephone contact.

You find the problem by means of the customer's voice, but you deal with it in terms of his physical situation.

Consider the customer to be in the palm of your hand, ready to be directed, but remember that he sees himself as being far away and easily cut off.

So put some physicality into your own conversation—weather, clothes you're wearing, the color of the rug on the floor—to give yourself reality. . .but relate consistently to *his* physical reality, even if you don't have many hints about it. (*Never* forget that it's raining in Los Angeles, if he mentions it, for example; that's an event for him, and you should recall it at the end of the conversation.)

Check the weather in the morning paper, for a start. It's a simple thing, but think how surprised you'd be if someone called from 1,000 miles away and remarked on the temperature where *you* are (or the local football game). **You've got to project yourself physically into the customer's backyard.**

And never forget to ask that basic sales question: *Why aren't you buying?* If you haven't figured out what the problem is, go to the source. The customer knows why he isn't buying. Usually, he'll tell. Often, you can do something about it. You just need that clue to follow, when nothing is coming across the telephone line.

Or should you call it intermission, and try again later?

That's the subject of the next chapter.

CHAPTER FOUR
When to Call

ON THE HUNT FOR PROSPECTS CLOSE TO HOME

Even if you don't intend to make your pitch over the telephone, you have to develop your own script for scouting prospects in your town.

Obviously, you should look for other means of contact, when possible, because then you can bring all your talents to bear upon the prospect. But if he's busy, or you live in a large town, it may be that the telephone is the most direct approach.

You have to initiate. You have to state your business and lay it out on the line.

> *Your goal is not to make a sale,*
> *but to arrange a meeting.*

You have a "soft" assignment, in a sense. You're not asking that much of a commitment—just the consent to come in for a look-see.

On the other hand, make sure the casual arrangement has underpinnings of steel. This is just a visit to the shop, or the sales floor, but make sure that you have time and date down pat. Have it so certain—and repeat the particulars—that you won't be out of line to call later, in case your prospect doesn't show, and ask with concern what happened.

Concern, that is, not anger.

Your role in prospect calling is to make yourself available for discussion. You are trying to make opportunities happen.

CEMENTING A RELATIONSHIP

The best customers are the ones who have already bought from you. They will buy again.

The telephone is an intimate, casual and inexpensive way for you to build a long-term relationship with customers. You don't want to harass them, of course, but there are legitimate occasions for calling. A six-month checkup, or a special sale, or a sudden drop in interest rates—the reason will depend upon the product.

And you are, thanks to common sense, drawing a fine line between keeping the customer informed and suggesting that he become satisfied with what he recently bought. Your tactics for the life of the product are to check up on the performance and to offer help with service problems. Within a logical period of time, you may begin suggesting—not that he *replace*—but that he *upgrade*. It's not that the first product is falling apart; it's that he is in a position to appreciate a better item.

In certain circumstances, it is even appropriate to call with condolences when there is a death in the family, or with congratulations, if the event is really special and publicly known.

Remember: *You are usually calling a family, not just one person.* You're tying up the line, if only for a few minutes, so you better make sure you don't waste anyone's time. You ought to find out when most people in your customer's social class and neighborhood are likely to eat, or watch a big game, or go to evening church services. Always remind yourself of the obvious. You are trying to make yourself memorable, not an annoyance. Keep those ears wide open for the unspoken news that you are calling at a bad time. Hit and run, that's the idea. Say your piece, cover the embarrassing silences and leave while they're waiting for more.

WHEN THERE'S NO OTHER WAY

In some sales situations, the telephone is the only possible instrument of communication.

How do you start? This depends upon the importance of your prospect. As we've already suggested, Power Phoning is fueled by research beforehand, when it's going to pay off. You're a voice from the void, but you should know as much as you can about who you're calling and what he probably needs. You should know something about his town and the way life is lived there. Most importantly, you should have a very good idea, before ever lifting up the receiver, about just how well your services are going to mesh with the needs of the prospect.

All right, you can't always know all of these things. But you can come closer than most salespeople do, if you view that phone call as the climax of a campaign— not the whole enterprise.

You've got to build up to the phone
call, just as you would prepare
yourself to enter a customer's office.
Same process exactly.

You've got to have a game plan in mind. You've got to buoy yourself up to a peak of self-confidence. You've got to *know* that you are on top of the situation. Some people even feel more professional if they are sitting up straight at the desk, tie carefully knotted, as if they can be seen. Yes, that can help. *But it shouldn't distract you from the real appearance, the appearance of your voice.*

Do you gargle? Spray your throat? Run over a few scales? Well, none of this could hurt. The real secret to a strong voice, though, the kind that impacts across the wires, is very simple—and, we're sorry to say, like most secrets to success, it takes some work. **Voice teachers agree that the principal ingredient in a winning voice is good health.** If you've lost sleep the night before, you might be able to smile yourself through an interview, and few will be the wiser. But it shows in your voice.

So, with your voice in good order, and all your sales preparations run down the checklist, the problem now is . . . getting heard.

GETTING HEARD

Have you prepared the way?

Red-carpet calls: In some situations, you should have sent materials ahead, or warned your prospect by letter or telegram that you would be making a telephone call.

Another route is to call his receptionist or secretary, but don't ask to talk to him. You're making telephone *appointments,* and think that the two of you will need at least ten minutes (or whatever) for a worthwhile discussion. Can she book you? If she won't be specific, try to find out a ball-park time slot, and ask her to pass along the information that you will be calling that particular day. (Naturally, you don't carry this approach past logic; if he's available when you're on the line, you *will* talk with him.)

This type of preparation makes the points you always want to make:

- That you're organized
- That you don't have time to waste and don't intend to waste anyone else's time
- That you are in control of your schedule—and are probably in control of a lot more than that.

Have you prepared yourself? As we've suggested, research is crucial, to the extent that it can be carried out. Information about the customer and his company, about his hobbies and his professional ambitions— well, these would be terrific.

Often you have to punt; we realize that. But you can prepare yourself to talk with the "customer-as-type"— not to belittle his individuality, but to play to those ideas and qualities that are representative of someone in his position.

You may not be able to find out anything about the customer as an individual human being, but you can probably get your hands on a trade publication that he would read. You may not be able to find out much about the actual operation of his plant, but you can find out about similar operations.

And, with an ear alert to the need for a quick rewrite, you have your script in hand . . . and have tested it for telephone viability. You know what points you want to make, and you have broached them to yourself on the tape recorder we mentioned earlier. You've learned which of your pet phrases really come across with power and class, and which get lost somehow in transmission. You've decided how you want to sound, on this occasion. *You are, in the best of all possible worlds, ready to make this telephone call in your sleep.*

Have you *un*prepared yourself? Don't overdo it. If your customer doesn't want to talk about the day's stock market, don't rush ahead and show off your knowledge about gold futures. *Control your preparation; don't let it control you.*

Don't make assumptions that can insult your customer and ruin your image of control: Don't assume that he is married, and certainly don't assume that he refers to his wife as the "little woman" or his receptionist as "my girl." If there's just been an election in his state, don't assume that you know his views or could even take a stroll through the land mines offered by a discussion of the issues involved.

You are using your preparation to control the course of a conversation the way a race-car driver controls his highly tuned machine: on top of the steering wheel and the foot pedals with a vengeance, but listening every second for unusual sounds in the motor and chassis.

You have to be ready to draw upon your preparation, but you don't flaunt it. *You're not on the phone to tell the man what he already knows. And you're certainly not there to let him know that you think you're going to educate him.*

How's your timing?

Not only should you know when to hang up, you should know when to call again. Don't leave this critical information hanging. Ask. Make a definite appointment, to the extent that you can. If you can't name the date and the time, at least get something like "within the month" or "right after the election." Politely tell the customer that, yes, that sounds fine and you are marking it down in your appointment calendar.

To strengthen that call, give yourself and the customer an "assignment," so that each of you is working on it, already something of a team. It should be something simple, and it can be either personal or business in orientation. Say that you'll find out for certain if a certain quarterback really went into retirement in your town and opened a restaurant—assuming that some such question arose out of conversation. Or have your customer promise to find out the name of a certain product that failed for him, or the exact number of feet available for putting your equipment in place.

The less important, the better. This is just a way of tagging you and your upcoming call in the memory. **Rather than the person who will call again from Company X, you are the human being who had an interest in a specific thing, or could answer a trivial**

question for him. This is a kind of commitment to the next phone call.

And no Power Phoner needs to be told, at this point, that you should not only have the information he wants —which shows that you come through, even in the little things—but you should have it ringed with diamonds, because you are the type who goes the extra mile. That is, you not only found out what the quarterback's doing these days, but you got his autograph and it's in the mail.

Do you need the blindfold, or shall we just fire? Stand up and take it—that's the other time when you should reach for the telephone, without a moment's hesitation.

When you come back to the office, and there's a message about a product complaint, or your mail has an angry letter, don't wait for the carrier pigeons. *Call. Call, and do everything you can do to rectify the situation. **If your company won't let you perform in this way, find another company fast.*** You can't be a Power Seller if you leave a trail of dissatisfied customers behind. They have phones, too. They have friends.

We live in an age of consumerism, and everyone you deal with knows that. If you're dealing in retail, your customers have a right to expect quick service, when something goes wrong. If you're dealing with business professionals, then you are dealing with men and women who have to respond to the challenges of the consumer movement, and they certainly expect to reap the benefits of it.

*Quite apart from the ethics, and
that is fundamental, it is always
good business to call back when
there's a complaint.*

You're going to come through anyhow, so why not
come through promptly and cheerfully? Don't act as if
you're making compensation at the point of a gun. It's
your job. It's your privilege. **You're in business to
make things work, not to leave a trail of failures.**
The intimacy and immediacy of a phone call will do
much to assuage the customer's sense of loss or incon-
venience, until compensation is actually made.

AFTERWORD

The phone sits there, a machine waiting for your touch to bring it to life.

But you can't consider it a machine. You can't look at it as an object in itself; *it is your connection with someone else.* Through it, you project an image based upon your voice, based on your personality, fortified with your sales preparation.

Each time you approach the phone for a sales contact, it has to be as much an event as an appointment in the flesh. You don't pick up the receiver until you're primed. *You are at all times aware of the person on the other end and his situation.* If necessary, wear blinders or close your eyes; you have to be where he is, bringing yourself to his understanding.

At the same time, you have all the advantages of note taking and research available to you. You should keep notes from previous conversations, if you are calling someone a second or third time. You should have your files of correspondence in front of you, if you have been exchanging letters.

> *You should plan the phone call*
> *just as you plan a sales presentation*
> *to a group or a tough new prospect.*

You visualize your customer, and you try to imagine what images your conversation will bring to him. You can have written down in front of you the main points you want to make and remain determined to bring them up, when appropriate.

Afterword

> *The trick is to concentrate on the*
> *sound that goes over the wire...*
> *your voice, and its pauses. The*
> *words. The implications that lie*
> *beneath the words. The image in*
> *sound.*

Above all, don't let the telephone cause you to relax your businesslike manner. You can be casual and friendly, because that is surely the American Way of Business... *but you don't forget the purpose of your call:*

- Business should be taking place.
- Points should be made.
- Commitments should be made.
- Follow-ups should be scheduled.

Once you realize how to translate your Power Sales talents into the medium of the telephone, you'll understand that you already know how to sell over the telephone. **Power Phoning is just Power Selling with electronic aids.** Concentrate your efforts into beaming your talents into that tiny mouthpiece, and you will have the key to successful telephone sales.